The Dream Police

Also by Dennis Cooper:

The Dream Police

Selected Poems,

1969–1993

Dennis Cooper

Grove Press

New York

Published simultaneously in Canada
Printed in the United States of America

FIRST EDITION

Library of Congress Cataloging-in-Publication Data

Cooper, Dennis, 1953–
The dream police: selected poems, 1969–1993 / Dennis Cooper.
ISBN 0-8021-1569-1
I. Title.
PS3553.0582B69   1995   811'.54—dc20   94-39086

DESIGN BY LAURA HOUGH

Grove Press
841 Broadway
New York, NY 10003

10 9 8 7 6 5 4 3 2 1

Acknowledgments

Certain of these poems have appeared in the books *Tiger Beat* (Little Caesar Press, 1978), *Idols* (The Sea Horse Press, 1979; Amethyst Press, 1989), *The Tenderness of the Wolves* (The Crossing Press, 1981), *The Missing Men* (Am Here Books/Immediate Editions, 1981), *He Cried* (Black Star Series, 1985), and *Four Marines and Other Portraits: Photographs by Jack Shear* (Twelvetrees Press); in the magazines *Shiny International* and *Outweek*; on the PBS television program *The United States of Poetry* and on the syndicated series *Poetry Spots*; on *Prisons of the Flesh*, a musical collaboration with composer John Zorn and writer Casey McKinney; and in the anthologies *Uncontrollable Bodies: Testimonies of Identity and Culture* (Bay Press), *Postmodern American Poetry: A Norton Anthology*, *Gay and Lesbian Poetry in Our Time: An Anthology* (St. Martin's Press), *American Poetry Since 1970: Up Late* (Four Walls Eight Windows), *Out of This World* (Crown), *Poetry Loves Poetry* (Momentum Press), *The Son of the Male Muse: New Gay Poetry Anthology* (The Crossing Press), and *Coming Attractions: American Poets in Their Twenties* (Little Caesar Press).

I'm very grateful to Felice Picano, Tom Clark, John Gill, Peter Schjeldahl, Edmund White, Robert Glück, Bruce Boone, Walt Bode, Morgan Entrekin, Colin Dickerman, Ira Silverberg, Richard Haasen, Hudson, Mark Ewert, Casey McKinney, Linda Roberts, Joel Westendorf.

Contents

I. Dumb

'69–'78

for

Jerene Hewitt

Ron Koertge

Bert Meyers

After School,
Street Football,
Eighth Grade

Their jeans sparkled, cut off
way above the knee, and my
friends and I would watch them
from my porch, books of poems
lost in our laps, eyes wide as
tropical fish behind our glasses.

Their football flashed from hand
to hand, tennis shoes gripped
the asphalt, sweat's spotlight on
their strong backs. We would
dream of hugging them, and crouch
later in weird rooms, and come.

Once their ball fell our way
so two of them came over, hands
on their hips, asking us to
throw it to them, which Arthur did,
badly, and they chased it back.
One turned to yell, "Thanks"

and we dreamed of his long
teeth in our necks. We
wanted them to wander over,
place deep wet underarms to
our lips, and then their white
asses, then those loud mouths.

One day one guy was very tired,
didn't move fast enough,
so a car hit him and he sprawled
fifty feet away, sexy, but he was
dead, blood like lipstick, then
those great boys stood together

on the sidewalk and we joined them,
mixing in like one big friendship
to the cops, who asked if we were,
and those boys were too sad to counter.
We'd known his name, Tim, and how
he'd turned to thank us nicely

but now he was under a sheet
anonymous as God, the big boys crying,
spitting words, and we stunned
like intellectuals get, our high
voices soft as the tinkling of a
chandelier on a ceiling too high to see.

The School Wimp

In high school
I lived against walls,
hushed in dope deals.
My friends: my victims
moped around me
like a weak species.

He used to stand out
like a girl thrown
into our locker room,
a slim novel pressed
to his ribs, horn rim
ships docked at his eyes.

I floated above him,
a prize for cute babes
who shared the
dagwood of my wallet.
Their small pink pouts
opened for chicken feed.

In college, I learned
I could read.
One by one I found
the books he'd pored over:
Mallarmé, Colette, Oscar Wilde.
I sat and perused, and
all my friends looked like him.

Then, after eight years
I see him in a bar.
But now his sort attracts me
and later, when the sun
slants into his home,
my hard cock pokes through
his smile like a cigar.

BL

When I see
a boy having
sex before
he even knows
what it is
I want to kill
the men who
paid his way,
who kiss his
bug-mouth
and poke
at his farts,
lean back from
him burping,
only attracted
when a boy
lies face down,
his eyes dull
like a midget's,
a boy leading
men, the same
guys who should
tell him to
get lost, scram,
when he teases
them, but who
aim at it, turn
fools in his
presence, as if
he were the

true love
ahead, and
not the wild
crush far behind

Boys I've Wanted

for Ian Young

Craig Tedesco

This smile knew
girls, kissed
mother and burgers.
This smile was
turned against me;
"Hey asshole,"
it grinned. This hair
was red, and face
tanned by freckles.
No beard dimmed this chin.
These eyes had
never seen breasts
or cunt, though
this smile said
they had. This smile
spit in textbooks,
farted behind
old backs, dared me
to start something.

In my dreams
these eyes clenched
beneath me.
This smile was bound,
or not a smile,
or it was softened
and smeared by mine.

This hair was tousled
and these shoulders
white. Hands and lips
knew them. This head
was thrown back.
This boy loosened, was God.
Neck filled the frame.

Greg Tomeoni

I was in eighth grade
when he was in seventh.
He bought Dylan the same day
I did, and wanted
to sleep with me (he called
it frigging), so we tried.
His breath was of hamburger
and I licked his teeth
when he kissed me.
He held my wrist,
serious as a doctor.
He was dark and Italian, energetic
and long-haired. He liked
his boys tall and thin, like him.
I was the first of millions, he said.
I remember our position,
side by side, and the quick pulse
of our breaths, sometimes
steady, sometimes off on their own
like two men racing.
I remember him saying he loved me
and that I thanked him
and that we didn't come (too young I think)
but grew bored of it around sunrise
turning back to back, smoking,
filling the room with
a pale cloud, a food smell.
We slept in a hot blue night.

Scott Van Der Karr

It was the Christmas dance
wasn't it? My rock band
played. You joined the dance floor.
We had knocked over the big tree.
We had opened the mock packages.
Some of us were stoned, and
festooned our hair with the wrapping.
The stink of our two-bit colognes
filled the air, sweetest at the dancing.
It was light only in blemishes.
We were moving, that was all.
It vanished behind and ahead of us.
My band was the Stones. I, Jagger.
Your eyes were closed. You knew your way.
You wore an old pair of jeans
and fringe jacket tight
at the back, vague at the front.
Cocks didn't matter then.
It was ass we dreamed of, smooth as our ideas.
You knew how to wear yours.
Girls took it in their hands
when they danced. It rose through them;
it gripped their breasts;
it glowed out their eyes and mouths.
Though you were stoned
and stumbling, braying your words,
every girl schemed for you,
cute as you were, and steeped in blond.
Now my cock was up like Jim Morrison's,
your name mixed with Nadine's.
I sang the songs to you: the rough and

hard ones, the silky ballads.
Later I danced beside you, drunken,
stumbled into you again and again.
And I could smell your sweat and your breath.
Everyone could. Did you notice?

Mike Robarts

(page from a porno novel I wrote at sixteen)

and Keith was very drunk. Those beers had worked well. Stan pulled me aside and said one more beer and Keith couldn't fight off a feather. But that would take a little while and before then why didn't we do in his brother Mike. I'd been both worried and desirous for this moment all evening. Mike was my best friend and I loved him. The horror of killing him was as sexy an idea as I could imagine. He'd trust me all the way to the end. I suggested the pool and Stan thought that was a good idea. We moved back into the group. Mike was sitting back on the couch, relaxed, hands behind his head. The blue pants he always wore were tight in the crotch and my heart leapt when I realized whatever was there would soon be mine. I sat down beside him and suggested he and I go swimming in Stan's pool. He'd brought his trunks along in case and said yes. He got up and went into the bathroom to change. I had mine on under my jeans and just took everything off over them. Stan came up to me and said he'd swim too and that we'd grab him together, me at the head and he at the feet, strip him and get what we wanted and drown him. He said Dave would help us if we needed him. Mike came out of the bathroom in his trunks: tight blue swimmer's silks, the ones we had to wear at school. He looked so good. He smiled at me and we went out to the pool. Stan dove in and then Mike did. I followed. We raced the length a few times, then stood in a circle in the shallow end breathing hard. Stan glanced at me. This was to be the moment. I was shaking with excitement and nervousness. I said to Mike he was beautiful. He looked embarrassed and said not to be weird. I reached for him, my hands slid around his slippery brown waist and I kissed him on the lips. He got mad and pulled away. Stan grabbed him and held him against me, his head steady, and I licked all over his face. Mike was pissed off and yelling for me to stop. I ran my hand down into the front of his trunks and pushed them off. I felt him there and squeezed his balls. Stan had to hold him really hard because he was struggling furiously. While he did Stan chewed at his ear. I told Stan to turn him around and he did. There was his ass. I felt it and opened it. I licked down his back and all over his buns. I spanked him hard and shoved my finger up the hole. Stan said, "Let's kill him." I started hitting Mike on the back as hard as I could. He was screaming. Stan put a finger up Mike's nose and pushed it hard to one side breaking the nose. Stan turned him around and I hit him wildly in the chest and belly. I slapped his blood-smeared face over and over. Then we pushed him under the water. We held him there and he struggled. Soon he was still. I carried him to the pool deck and kissed his dead mouth and put my cock up his cool quiet ass again and again. I told myself I was glad I was drunk.

Ed Hong

When they snapped his picture
he was on LSD
and flunking everything.
You would have said:
"beautiful loser,
good for a rape and an OD."
You would have jerked off once
and been done with him. His friends did.
But you should have seen him
when a Christian smile
licked these lips.
Four months after this photo
his fists softened like swallowed pills.
His harangue calmed to lectures,
the Word, the Book
tucked in an underarm.
Hair fell to his shoulders
and filled with hands,
girls', friends', parents', God's.
We let him blather about love,
a world one thought beyond us,
the day we would float.
We didn't argue or contradict.
His chin rose like the hour hand.
We listened. We let
him have whatever made him
this way and this good.

Mark Clark

walked with his hands
near his hips
like he wore guns
and was Wanted
in fifty states.
Out of the blue
something would tick him
and he'd attack
a friend, a girl,
whatever was near,
his face dark
as a rag pushed
onto a wound.
He was so alive then;
you had to desire
his wildness, his looks.

Even the coaches
let him pound
and bought him beers afterwards
and wanted to run him
for a week, train him,
be the one to bring him down.
And I, too,
in my room at night
dreamt of taming him
with my body, my mouth
so wet he would drink from it
like a kid does a hose
when he has been running all day
and must stop, must drink.

Steve Nelson

The beauty I saw in
him was a cross
between Marilyn Monroe
and shade.
It shared my beers
and my sleep
through high school.
In those days
his thinness graced
every ball game
with its fumbling,
and his face
without a care.
I pointed him out to Lisa
and she wanted him
like a dog wants human hands
(her analogy).
She had an advantage,
being a girl,
and screwed her way
through his friends
("wimps and monsters")
to reach him one night
in the ruins of some party
when he was too drunk,
saw breasts in the fog of his eyes
and drooped to them
gulping back vomit.
She had to strip him down,
bite his cock hard,
bang his thin ass.

"Still, it was the best screw
ever . . . there could possibly be,"
she smiled
smoking his Marlboros.
My cock raged in my jeans,
attesting to the fact;
but, I begged to differ.

Bill McCall

Friends, see how pale
his skin was. It
glowed. And his lips
with a trace of teeth, and
ears like boats for tongues.

I'd fold my hands before
a nonsense God, asking
for his words and kisses.
I'd sob and spit his name
and live on an ounce of sleep.

I can't explain the ways
he moved in me, emptied and
filled me. I was crazy
and young, and more
in love than I'll ever be.

I used to say I'd give
my life for his,
wrote it in poems of shit worth.
As I jot this down now
I know it was true.

To this day I'll see
him somewhere, smiling my way,
deep in his life.
Then in this poem, this life,
my work lies deserted as a drunk's.

First Sex

This isn't it.
I thought it would be
like having a boned pillow.

I saw myself turning
over and over in lust
like sheets in a dryer.

My style was reckless,
wool dry. Other than mine
there were little or no arms.

I could whisper anything
into an implied ear
and praise would rise
like a colorless, scentless gas.
Then I would breathe to sleep.

But my lover moves.
And my lips grow numb as rubber
before I capture half the ass
that rose like Atlantis
from my dreams.

I try to get his shoulder blade between my teeth.
He complains, pillow in his mouth.
Doesn't mean it.
Means it.

He rolls onto his back,
face raw and wet as fat,
like it has been shaken from nightmares.
I don't know how to please this face.

Tomorrow when he has made breakfast
and gone, I will sweep
the mound of porno from my closet,
put a match to its lies.

I will wait in my bed
as I did before, a thought ajar,
and sex will slip into my room
like a white tiger.

A Boy Wins His Body

His toys and he are tied.
He rises, they move with him.
As rain with its cloud
slides, shadowing the field,
he darkens our rooms and us.

He is dirty wherever he
touches down, loves only
mud and running. Soon we slip
from his mind. An odd mood
draws him to the unexplored
cave, forces him to strip at

knife point, kisses him
in a rushing river. "Fuck!"
A great word needs to be
yelled. Running down the hill
his breath leaves his body
naked. The sun moves inside

like tea and he smiles.
Then winter ties him up indoors.
Books light his faces.
Coughing his one flu into
the soup, he dreams of friends
trapped in rooms dimmed

to reading and naps. He
strays in his sleep to where
dreams are clearing. He finds flesh
in his clouds, a boy hiding
'neath stairways, hand to cock,
grinning. Nothing so bright

in the water or sky. And
the boy joins in, teeth parted
and wet like the sheets where
he lies with a friend, cool butt
in his face. All he is worth.

My Grandmother Grows

I remember my grandmother
in her elegant fifties,
leaning above my toy bed, bent only
at the waist like Snow White.

Her best stories slipped a carousel
into my room. I rode it all day
then fell asleep, to the rain
of her small feet in the hall.

For years I dreamed of her,
wrote letters increasingly
short and typed, and grew up.
Now she's alone, so I open my doors.

Morning she flails from sleep
like a drowning girl;
some prince should lean there
complying like a day dream.

Days she sits over cold coffee
or lies in the dark,
or climbs the floors,
stooped as if in a cave.

At night I lead her into my room.
She tows the merry-go-round
but now it is xerox gray
and I drop right through it.

Lecture, 1970

I know men who would kill you for sitting in this room. From here you look dulled, like a hundred workers glancing up from the machines of your thinking. You put the fire out with your meals. The best people are thin, bones distorting their skin. You should be able to pick them out easily, tear off their shirts, get a firm grip around one rib, and rip. I know men who have thought about going that far. They are guys you could worship, usually blond. Blonds are an angelic race. It doesn't take acid to know this. When I was in Holland, every blond was in love with every other. Bouquets of them stood on the corners. They seemed above life. In Paris, people are as alive as if they've just been stabbed, as if they're running for help everywhere they go. You have to close your eyes after a while. You have to read about them. New York is sort of the same, but with death like a permanent night thrown over the place. The French wouldn't step over a dying drunk. They'd kick his mouth into a shoe and walk a block that way.

Here in Los Angeles we're halfway there. The highlights of some of your lives are dimmer than a French baby's dreams. You could wear a shirt that reads, "My existence on this planet is a total humiliation to me. End my life, please!" And some asshole would calm you down, slow you down. He'd ask you to sniff flowers and urinate for over a minute. In France you would die. They really live there. Men in the subways who lie behind money cups with their toeless feet propped up are either given a hundred francs or beaten. None of this "look away" shit. Nothing to stare at. Those guys are more alive than you could ever be. They want to die because they've peaked. They breathe the exhaust off the five o'clock train, the sweat off hurrying backs. Their lungs should be filled with robes. You and I should feel constant pain. We should die of cancer for sixty years. Childhood is free. You can float around until you're seventeen. Then your stomach will burn, or you will lose one hand in a light boating accident, or be paralyzed from the waist down.

A wise man told me that I'm wasting my life. I am. So are my friends. I have a friend whose mind could cure death, but he watches TV all day. He gave up. He should be killed. I'd do it, but there's a law. I'm caught by these things. You can say, "He'll get tired of lounging around," but he won't. I had a dream that I was going to die, which is obviously true. But I have not left these pages for my dreams. I cannot eat a hammer like Rimbaud did. It can't be done. What Rimbaud tried to do is a Bible. You and I should read it like we read Mario Puzo, not like we read Sade or Céline. It should breeze through our eyes. But we are not our younger brothers, thoughts deep in their clear brows. We are not pure. We cannot listen. Children would and should kill us. We could and won't nail a few of them to the walls. I want them around me all the time.

None of you will get out. Some of you may be brilliant. I haven't found you, and I won't gut myself so that brighter eyes open inches above yours. If you are young and beautiful, let's go to bed together while our asses still quench our jeans when we wear them tight, while we can worship our hair. In France old people are idols. In America they're not. Neither of us are right. The French may walk in the shadow of Lautréamont. The Dutch may drive clouds. None of us are right. What is right is that we walk toward lamps and eat animals. When we actually close our hands over lights and set plates in our toilets we will be honestly great. Until then the most religious thing to do is slobber at slenderer bodies, look twenty all our lives. No matter what we do we will not poison the air or each other. We'll get used to it. We cannot, like the French, live so strongly that we're constantly putting out fires on our arms. So let's stand children on our shoulders and walk into the Century Plaza Hotel, and let's be greeted by gods.

Two Guys

One

these two are young whores who work the same beat
the one on his back is nineteen and a big seller
the other does alright but doesn't have his friend's looks
this is where the one on his back sleeps
the other guy comes by to visit when he's not busy
it's partly lust and partly loneliness that led them to this
the licker's name is marty
the other's name changes every three weeks:
scotty, tim, robin, mark, and steve (currently)
they've both been fucked countless times and like it
steve smokes marlboros constantly in fact one's gripped in his left
    hand
there is something of religion in their joining
marty thinks of steve's ass as an altar
he has just seconds ago lifted that leg and seen it
he is sniffing the great smell there
steve is devastated because he is totally revealed
even the stink of his ass has been discovered
the idea someone would lick there gives him cold chills
in a moment his other leg will be bent back and tongue worm
        way up inside him
at that point he will say he loves marty
in a way they are in love with each other
both are from the mid-west and were beaten by their fathers
neither of them can read more than street signs
marty is at the point where he'd kill for steve
steve senses this and they stick together, sometimes sell as a duo
both of them are thinking of nothing but steve's ass
marty is saying "christ you're so good so good"

you can hear the cars cruise Selma Street just outside this
    crash pad
they could be making a bundle tonight but they're busy
after this they'll go for dinner and taste each other in the
    food
marty will say "nothin tastes as good as your ass"
steve will laugh nervously and rub the back of his tight
    jeans
the sun will be up by the time they drop asleep
there are men who would give them a hundred each just
    to hold a camera on this sex
they don't know that though and it's great sex regardless.

Two

the hard hat came to this restroom to get sucked off or suck some
     good looking young stud
he scored pretty well and the other guys are envious
this stud's twenty-two and pretty well built too
hard hat asks the stud what a guy like him's doing here
"same thing you are" he says
the hard hat's in his late thirties, married, two daughters
but he can't get the smell of young men out of his head
so he comes here and does pretty well sometimes, like now
hard hat asked the stud to turn around for a while and he did
one thing's for sure this stud has a great ass
loosen it up a little with the tongue then fuck it
the stud's in the navy
"they let you in with that long hair?"
"sure they changed all that years ago"
this is just small talk and they forget it instantly
this stud likes to be eaten out from behind
it's one of hard hat's favorites too so he gives him a good cleaning
they don't even consider kissing, too swish
"hey man you had enough back there? fuck it already"
hard hat stands and works it up
pretty easy, though the stud's ass is nice and tight
he tells the stud so and the stud says he knows
"you must get it a lot on board"
"whenever i feel like it i guess"
hard hat comes in the asshole of the stud then the stud jacks off on
     the floor
when the stud's dressing the hard hat looks him over
the guy's really good, really well built

the hard hat wonders what it'd be like to cut a chunk
        outta those buttocks and eat it
he's half tempted to try it and fingers his knife
he could kill this kid and drag him off saying he's sick
        then do whatever he wanted and cook the meat
over a fire and eat it, do anything
no, might as well let him live
but thinking about this he's hard again
the stud says so long and so does the hard hat and that's it
hard hat sits here waiting for another guy to take this new
        load
the guy who comes to the stall is young, twenty-four
        probably, but nothing to look at and skinny as shit
what the fuck might as well let him suck him off
the kid gets down on his knees and whispers in a high
        voice something about getting down on his big
daddy or something
christ a god damn fairy but fuck might as well let him
hard hat breathes out and looks at the ceiling

Three

up top is ted, thirteen, french
below is jeff who's fourteen and french
they are in a hotel in paris
they are being paid to do this, to be photographed
ted is the boy the photographer wanted and his friend came along
this is not to say he's a dog
but the boy up top, he's the real find
the photographer's in his forties
he tells the boys what to do and they do it
it took ted a while to get into it but now he loves it
jeff seems to have done this before, really expert
first they stripped each other and sucked cocks
there is a good amount of kissing all through
while this is being taken the photographer's assistant is sucking
    jeff's ass off camera
the boys keep cracking up and the photographer shoots around
    that
if these pictures are going to sell they have to look serious
a boy must be worshiping another boy's body
he asks his assistant how the jeff boy's ass tastes
his assistant lifts his eyebrows without stopping sucking
when this is over the photographer can get some
but ted is the boy he's after
the boys go to the same school in the clichy area
they wanted money and went to stand in front of le drugstore
it didn't take them ten minutes to be purchased
they did this once before but were only jacked off and not before
    a camera
when this particular act is over jeff will pretend to be fucking his
    friend but it's easy to fake
no way, ted said, will he be buttfucked, not for a million francs

it will end with jeff exhausted in orgasm on ted's back
they will pretend to be asleep and satisfied
then the bright lights will go out and the boys will ask
     for their money
if they want their money they have to give a little more
they have no choice so they say yes but they won't like it
the photographer starts to suck ted's ass and yes it's
     delicious
he gets way up inside, stretching it until it takes four
     fingers to the third knuckle
jeff is getting similar treatment on the floor
the photographer kisses ted with the stink still on his lips
he bends ted back and up until he's open like a cave there
his fingers slide up and are licked as they come out
ted is just a nice looking french kid but this man is
     treating him like jeanne moreau never was
ted's just waiting for his money
this is no skin off his back but no big thrill either

Four

when johnny's father said they were going to europe for the
      summer he begged and prodded until his friend bill could
      come along
this is why
john's the one on his knees with the unusual taste
bill's the one getting it royally
the family is in amsterdam
everyone else is on the sight seeing tour
john and bill said they weren't feeling well
the fifth of gin on the table is almost empty, inside them
the sight seeing tour will take five hours
john thought about doing this to bill since he first saw him in gym
      class at school
they're both sixteen, clever and good-looking
he used to throw things and make bill bend over so he could get
      an idea of what it was like in there
he doesn't remember where he got this idea but a long time ago
bill's laughing but you can't hear him
it's a laugh because of his weird position and embarrassment
john is incredibly serious, and always is during this
they have done experiments in this area
john made bill eat just pizza for two days to see if the taste
      changed, then just indonesian food
he noticed differences, though slight, but there
bill had the runs for three days but john still did it, carefully
bill's content to suck john's cock though he thinks maybe today
      he'll try this on john
john keeps raving about it, there must be something to it
john talks to bill about them living together forever
bill is naive and lighthearted and says yes to that

when they walk down the street somewhere john drops
       back a few paces to see bill's ass move in his jeans
when there's any chance at all his hand's there fingering
if john's parents walked in it'd be curtains for him
they are the kind of people who'd send him to an insane
       asylum if his father didn't kill him first
john's taking a chance but he's a desperate kid
bill loves him in the way a young girl loves a boy
john's love for bill contains violence and obsession
but now his hands touch the smooth taut flesh and his
       tongue goes in as far as it can
he feels the breath of bill's light laughter on his thighs
the head of his cock rests in bill's soft beatle hair
bill's firm legs are around him
nothing comes into him nothing touches him but bill

Idol Is Available

First he's on television
winning the Emmy
then he's twenty feet off
to take an award while
I applaud and smile.

Since he came to light
a massive invasion
of awe filled my life,
taking more of my love
than a boyfriend; I

hung his pictures around
me, flushed with this
or that success, in nude
photos slipped out of
Germany, on magazine lids.

Shaun checked the stuff
over, blanched, said he'd
met the guy at parties,
said he was boring but
if I really wanted

he'd whisk me along
to evenings where I'd
put Him behind me, past
the fan letter foreplay
so magic at this point,

'cause Shaun's a star now,
has slipped himself into
the light from our mutual
dreaming, knows the guys
we once knelt before

hands to melting hearts,
and as *his* friend I could
join him, them, in that
cool distant cluster of
stars in a million eyes.

Well it's happened and
Shaun wasn't lying. By the
end of the evening just his
sex lured me and by morning
not even that, waking,

his skinny arm across
my chest, his bad breath on
my mind. I know every-
thing about my idol and
he's nothing like a god.

Swimmer

When a small girl
explores the lake with a mask
she rubs against Eric,
months there
gliding the depths,
arms straight out like a plane.
His trunks nine times too small.

Now when he drifts ashore
girls will put out their eyes
rather than toss him
a look like dreaming.

Monday Dave calls me
at a party,
kissing my stupid mouth
with the news.

As I wake Tuesday
I lie for hours
thinking of death,
then push myself to my cold feet.
When men pull Eric
out of the lake
the water follows him up
like a long gown.

Dean Corll

Corll worked hard,
took real chances,
and was rewarded
to wake from his dreams
within them,
as sated as runaways
at home under drugs.

The boys he wanted
too much, his.
The backs of small pants,
so mysterious,
more than a brilliant idea,
opened for him
wider than his palm.

Hot moist thighs
and wrists were his.
Skulls lost like
treasure chests beneath
soft hair, his.
Crying and tantrums, his.
Secrecy, timing, his
     alone.

The dead boy, loose
as a sack, could
be thrown over his shoulder
or against the wall.
This thought rose
like a genie from
the first boy he rubbed.

David Cassidy Then

David Cassidy picks me on *The Dating Game*.
I walk around the partition
and there he is. A quick kiss,
then Jim Lange gives us the good news.

"David, we'll be flying you and your date
to . . . Rio de Janeiro! You'll be
staying at the luxurious Rio Hilton
and attend a party in your honor!"

At the Hilton we knock the chaperone
out with a lamp, then we jive
around, smoke a little Colombian.
David says something to let me
know he's willing, and I get
to chew his clothes off.

He dances *Swan Lake* naked
and I sprawl out on the bed.
He saunters over scolding me in French,
and covers my face with his modest rear.

He gives me a few minutes
then he's up, blow-drying the drool
from his legs. He slips on a white jumpsuit,
runs a thumb across his teeth, and
turns to where I sit, still dreamy on the bed.

"Come on," he says, full of breath.
Never so proud, I bring my hands up,
rub his stink into my face like a lotion.
I will wear it to the party!

As the lobby doors open
reporters start the sea of lights.
The cameras take us kissing, dancing.
They angle to get David's sheathed body.
Girls watch his ass like a television screen
of men stepping onto the moon.

Little do they know what really lies there,
that this is no tan. "This is David,"
I say, smelling my face like a flower,
and pull him close, stoned out of my gourd.

From "Some Adventures of John Kennedy Jr."

The Murder

He remembers
putting a hand to his head,
the squiggle of his thoughts;

remembers his mother
was wasted, being bored,
a million tears.

When he talks about it
he goes way overboard.
My dad was a god, John says.

All he knows is what
we tell him, what he reads.
What he remembers is a big guy.

In New York

It's hot, and smoggy as Mars outside
so he stops for an ice cream
in the nearest Wil Wright's
and the clientele goes apeshit.

A man who loved his father
gives him his place in line, next!
John asks for a double;
he gets eight scoops and a real smile.

Then he starts up the boulevard
turning every head.
A filthy breeze blows his Beatle
bangs straight back.
He's famous, even without them.

Now let's stay with a couple
John has passed by
and overhear their reaction.
But it's awestruck, clichéd,
and not worth remembering.

In London

Jackie gives him
£10 for the day
and he cabs to Soho,
gambles half,
buys a coupla records
(Steely Dan and the Ramones)
and dips in a Wimpy's
to fill up his waist.

This side of the sea
missed Kennedy fever,
and John breezes by, dim
as the punk he resembles.

The only ones
who recognise him
are some gays,
and they just give low whistles
as he passes
and dream of making him
in a different world.

Taking a Self-Survival Course

Men boat him to an island
so moist it seems to have risen
like a big bathing cap from the waves.
John bites down on his tongue
and shivers through his blue Cardin.

They leave him pale and girlish
on the skinny beach, with his
handful of matches, plant book,
and smoldering Kennedy eyes,
talking their big stupid heads off.

Night drops fast. He sleeps under
dead leaves; his hair grows foul
as the malty earth. Next day he strips
to underwear, makes himself a leaf
crown, and by Thursday joins the beasts.

When the boat returns on Monday
it finds a boy to be reckoned with,
cured of cigarettes and snobbery.
The men clap him on the back like
he's choking, fierce in their affections.

John squats down with the other new men,
all so proud they haven't washed.
On the distant N.Y. dock he spots Jackie
and the reporters, happy as uncles to see him.
Finally he has something to tell them.

In School

When the professor tells his class
their homework is to write poems,
young John brings down his fist.
"But tonight the Knicks are playing Boston!"
He'll have to give his front rows away.

Instead he slogs through poets,
hates them all until William Carlos Williams.
"You mean this is poetry?" He leaps
on his notebook. "I can write this stuff
by the ton." And so he does, a twenty pager.

It's about his own brief life,
praise for the sports stars, shit for the press,
close shots at his deep dark family.
The next day he's graded on his reading;
John's poem is "I'm Going Nowhere":

"I never thought anyone died,
especially not me,
then my father and uncle got it from maniacs
and Ari kicked the bucket the hard way,
and I've started thinking of my own death,
when will it come and how,
by some madman out to end the Kennedys?
I hope so, and that it happens
before I have a chance to show my mediocrity.
I know that's clumsy rhythm
but what have I got to lose, man? . . ."

When John gets to these last words
tears shake his sullen reading.
Amazed, the professor looks straight
through John's tough punk texture,
and then an A+ flies John's way
like a fastball, or a perfect pass.

JFK Jr. to Play Father in Film

The producer wanted Mark Hamill
but the real thing will do.
Besides, the publicity's helpful.
So he catches John in a school play,
sees potential, is attracted,

takes the boy for a screen test.
John is shy. John is arrogant.
He is used to the cameras.
His average mind gives energy
but no more. He is playing

it slapstick. Then they go
for a beer. The producer would rather
sleep with him than cast him.
But how do you broach a Kennedy?
A big producer too is in awe

of them, even bit players. He
tries to relax, but drink after
drink the boy looks closer to
godhead, the scene more hopeless;
John's eyes tail every woman.

Then, to shake himself, "John, do
you want to play your father?"
"It's better than playing his son."
A bad joke, a bad moment that
the producer sees and John doesn't.

Then John rises, shakes hands.
The producer sees him go. He thinks,
"Nice ass but nothing upstairs," and
sits back, imagining sex, knows John's
sperm would taste like *something*.

II. Deaf

'78–'83

for

Amy Gerstler

Then as Before

It was Saturday morning, so I could sleep in. But my body, used to the call of the high school, spaced on at 7:15 and wouldn't be snuffed out again, no matter how much I yawned, on my stomach or back. So I propped a pillow behind me, sat up, and let my eyes clear on the poster from Alain Resnais' *Providence*, hung on the back of my bedroom door. It was my favorite film. It held the right combination of smarts and emotion—starring the first, with a cameo by the latter. When I established myself as an artist and was handed a sizable budget, I'd do something like it.

On the top shelf of my bookcase, a neat row of film cans made up my oeuvre. I was still proud of maybe a third. I'd been making small epics since I was thirteen, when I'd ridden around on my Stingray bike shooting montages of where I hung out. I still tried to watch them and see where I'd been. I peered through the premature, wobbly art, and they were trailers for my childhood, starring some friends who'd gone on to be strangers to me.

I leapt out of bed. I yanked a shoe box from the closet and cannonballed back in the covers. In the box was a stack of photos of me, my family, and friends through my life. I dumped them out on the blanket and pawed through the mess for anything, anywhere, anyone special. There I was, climbing out of some swimming pool. I was about ten years old. The less perfect color gradations in those days made me look gold, though I'd always been pale or burnt red.

Further back still, in black and white, one eight-by-ten featured me and some friends around eight years of age. We posed in a pack outside an old theater (torn down since then), having just seen or about to see something. The photo's frame cut off below the marquee, so I couldn't tell what my tastes were like then. My friends looked like typical children, with faces too mushy to give a clue what they were thinking. I remembered I thought I could tell.

I almost knew this old world where the ornate tail end of my parents' Montclair (lower right corner) would speed down this avenue pointing at places I could still picture—a Ralph's Super-market, my lime-green grade school, my family's first Spanish-style home. I wanted to locate these other young fellows whose parents had dragged them to some Amnesiaville. But I could only squint at their faces beyond the grid of the photo, as if through the chain-link fence of a school yard, scanning that shrunken-up hiding place. Now I looked at the light on the photo, then out the window which threw it—a playground more teasing than this tiny, flashbulb-lit one I had come from. Then as before, I had no choice in the matter. I put on my clothes and went out there.

There

He stood alone in the shadow.
His hands and his shoes jutted
out of the dark, with some dope
smoke. The rest of his body was
vague but exact, like a hologram
glimpsed through thick glasses.

He had two or three friends who
took orders, strolled off, and
came back with treasures. His
calm seemed as great as the one
in cartoons so deep in his past
they'd grown soft and unlined.

It was enough. Punks, jocks,
everyone watched him, pictured
him sprawled at a desk, clothes
torn apart by ulterior powers,
his sneer smudged with girls'
kisses, boys' wet red fists.

Somehow one girl got to him,
towed him around. He leaned
on her body. They grew loaded
together, mouths swinging open,
and walked in a slight pas de
deux on the outskirts of things.

Now they linger behind their
old friends, wiser but slower,
hugging in backgrounds, staring
into some nowhere, their eyes
grey with rest and the kind of
lust only the bored can imagine.

They loll around in their
arms and the look on his face
makes both whisper, undress.
Then they touch where they've
always imagined, and it feels
so cold and impressive to them.

Being Aware

Men are drawn to my ass by
my death-trance blue eyes
and black hair, tiny outfit,
while my father is home with
a girl, moved by the things
I could never think clearly.

Men smudge me onto a bed,
drug me stupid, gossip, and
photograph me till I'm famous
in alleys, like one of those
jerk offs who stare from
the porno I sort of admire.

I'm fifteen. Screwing means
more to the men than to me.
I daydream right through it
while money puts chills on
my arms, from this to that
grip. I was meant to be naked.

Hey, Dad, it's been like this
for decades. I was always
approached by your type, given
dollars for hours. I took a
deep breath, stripped, and they
never forgot how I trembled.

It means tons to me. Aside
from the obvious heaven
when coming, there's times
I'm with them that I'm happy
or know what the other guy
feels, which is progress.

Or, nights when I'm angry,
if in a man's arms moving
slowly to the quietest music—
his hands on my arms, in my
hands, in the small of my back
take me back before everything.

Wednesday

"The point is to touch them," a coach says, and eyes the young men on the field. They're throwing balls, looking around for directions. He lifts one big hand and waves it at them. "Hold your horses!"

". . . and in doing so make them grow up," frowns another. He's been in the war, seen how boys either cut it or don't in the big time. "One fall on their asses won't rape them."

Off a short distance, girls flop around in their sweatshirts and shorts, sprawled on the basketball court doing sit-ups, to disco. Their eyes are calmer than boys', especially turned to one another. They talk about creeps, those on the field for example.

The girls' coach is tired of their laziness. They'll do the exercise right, and with vigor. Her whistle clicks in her teeth, then squeals until all eyes are hers. "Now," she says, "let's get going. Lie on your backs . . . bend your legs up . . . and touch them."

When a single bell rings the boys and girls drop what they're holding, rush into two dressing rooms, slide out of blue shorts, and shout. Some trot to the showers. A few are too nervous to bathe in front of the others.

At the far end of the boys' locker room an open door leads to an office. Inside, coaches are wrestling. One of them leans in the doorway. A naked kid raps to him, voice full of reverence and fear. The coach keeps his gaze on the ceiling. Anything the boy says is so moving.

The student, Steve Behr, is stupid but handsome. At this point he pulls it off. His parents adore him, and friends run the gamut from poets to robbers. "A nice guy," they say when girls ask what The Behr's like. "He's decent."

Both Jocelyn and Brenda, two lanky blondes, like Steve. In their locker room they dash to the showers, side by side, talking about him. Joc loves his haircut and Bren thinks his peak was last summer, so suntanned they hardly could recognize him. He said "Hi" to them, real intensely.

The boys' coaches know what Steve has and hasn't. He's a good-looking boy and a friendly guy. Fine at athletics, tries hard. They notice him sprawled in the showers. He sees them staring and grins, but he can't imagine their feelings. Some asshole just slugged him and he fell down on his ass. But by this time it's nothing.

Grouped outside the gymnasium, students wait for the bell to ring. Then they meet their friends at the usual places. Druggies stroll toward the restrooms. Jocks jog by the bleachers. Girls are scattered among and beyond them.

When Steve looks at the girls he doesn't know what to do. So, he has picked a lover from those who are like him, for whatever reason. They meet up and walk toward the street as a couple, Keds flattening the grass. The yellow buses open their doors and students climb in. Windows fill up with steam.

At home Steve's mother works in the garden all day, and waits for her son. Or she cleans up the house, or looks out a window. Her breath leaves a cloud on the glass. Now she sees him come walking up the black driveway, scanning the place till he spies her. The look on her face is familiar.

They meet in the kitchen—she with her coffee cup, he with a spoon draped in ice cream. She lays her day out on the table. He mentions his between swallows, then jumps on his gold ten-speed bike and whizzes down Fair Street to a friend's house, as he has every Wednesday since grade school.

Kevin's parents have money. Their backyard is like arboretums that Steve has been bused to on field trips and, in its damp depths, as shady as though it's been tinted in grey, the gardener's storeroom sits open. Once inside it, Steve draws out a joint from his wallet, lights its tip, lets it simmer a second, then slurps the smoke down. He hands it to Kevin.

When the small room is clouded and their tension's snuffed like the cherry, they strip and lie out on the cold cement floor, cocks nearly branding each other. Then Steve pulls away and they shoot their white loads on the ground.

They smear it around with their heels, and slip back into tee shirts plus jeans. Kevin's shirt says, "Surf Life!" on its chest and Steve's holds the colored-in face of a rock star who both of them worship. They wish they could kiss him right now.

While walking back to the mansion, Kevin looks in Steve's eyes. They're just calm, nothing special. Now the house is in sight and a woman leans out of a lower right window, watching the sunset. "Staying for dinner?" she calls out to Steve. Kevin asks him more gently. "Okay," Steve whispers, then cups his mouth with his hands. "Okay!"

John Kennedy Jr.
Faces the Future

"Well," he says, "What's ahead?"
and wipes Michelob from his chin.
His friends nod, drunker than he is.
He has been blathering for hours.
". . . and where will *I* be, you know?
Parents and all that, just bore me."

Someone suggests a political office.
"Too obvious," he says. How about
a race car driver? "I haven't got
the guts." An actor. "Well, maybe."
A writer. "Slight possibility." A
lawyer. "Those guys are assholes."

The girl in his arms says, "Be
practical. As long as you have
wealth you can just lounge around.
Why fuck with your legend? All
this talk is boring. It doesn't
get you anywhere. It's bullshit."

John stands up from the table,
walks outside alone. "Let him go,"
a pal mumbles. He strolls through
the streets of Hyannis, wandering,
thinking. He is so alone in this.
No one else could ever understand.

He wants to read his name outside
the society column, find people who
will notice *him*. But his thoughts are
messy, too drunken, and he sits down
on a remote park bench, his big wavy
head in hands, the whole world in them.

Hustlers

for Jerry Patterson

Two beers screw my head up.
I lean back against a dark wall.
My long hair drifts in my eyes.
Let's say the moon makes a decision.
I land the corner legend surrounds.
I say more than I pretend to.
I prefer to be fucked to The Beatles.
I stand with the guys I resemble.
Jerry, Tom, Dick, Sam, Julian, Max, Timmy.
Guess which of those names is perfect.
We dream of a casual million.
We light our cigarettes gently.
I take what the night has to offer.
I roll a ripe peach from one wrist to the other.
I can't speak I'm so fucking stupid.
Our bodies are simply stupendous.
When we breathe, it takes us apart.
You know. You're inside us.

For Mark Stephens

My mother drank, and she sat
in a house the size of the Hilton
in one small room, at a black
grand piano, through cigarette
smoke, by a dinner so old it
cracked like dried mud. A tune
created her mood. Some whim
was letting her play the same
exercise seventeen times. She
had been smart in the Fifties.
She was not handsome, but she
was composed, made me between
vodkas. My room was up one
or more of the stairways, left
down the hall, left again. I
knelt here, twisted a knob, and
rock music rose genie-like in
the room, gripped me and took
me away. I'd leap in my room,
hand strumming my belt like a
rock star, lip-synching what
hid my new thoughts in my body.
When my sister split, there
were places to hide in the
mansion. Piles of her junk
became far distant planets.
I couldn't quite build a
transporter, though I hung up
black lights, sheets over
lamps, played songs at half-speed.

I thought if I darkened
the room, blurred sofas, sat
there, that might be heaven,
controlled by one light switch
like LSD hinted. Hearing a
song, I went up. Downstairs
my mother got drunk all alone.
Knowing that I was nearby she
would wobble to the piano,
plop down, and play the one
piece she learned from lessons,
her body bent forward, with
spit on her lips, eyes shining.
The melody rose through her
clutches, was part of the world
that corraled where even her
hands couldn't snuff it. The
music passed through the ceiling
to where I'd crouch dreaming,
host to the tingle of darkness.
It touched in a way I couldn't
shrug off. Doped, far away
from my life, I listened, and
it reached out and caressed me.

My Past

for Jim Stegmiller

is a short string of beautiful
boys or young men I admired,
dragged to bed, left in ruins
on corners with taxi fare home.
Another of friends who were
horny, who I could have slept
with but didn't because they
were ugly, insane, or too much
like me to be sexy. We were
partners for sweeps of wild
parties, took dope till they felt
like museums which we
could pick over for bodies
to idealize with caresses.
The sun rose slowly. I was
still huffing and toiling
with them, like a sculptor
attempting to get things just
right—finally collapsing
in bed with some smeared,
smelly torso before me, and
a powerful wish to be left
alone. Take you, for example,
who I found throwing up in
the bathroom of some actor's
mansion and crowned my new
boyfriend. Your ass made me
nervous till I explored it.
Now I want to forget it. My

friends feel this way too.
I know them. We've been close
since before we were artists
working to leave haunted eyes
on our lovers. I've thrown
out hundreds like you, and
found only art can remain so
aloof in its makeup that I'll
stare endlessly into its eyes
like a kid with a microscope.
Once I was back when art chatted
just over my head, when I was
still glancing up the red swim
trunks of some boy who I think
was named Jimmy, and wondering
what could be out there, miles
from my hands. He was leaving
like you. Who knows where that
man and that feeling are now.

For My Birthday

After much talk and laughter
friends are buying a whore,
one I couldn't worm from
the bars with a toothy smile.
He will be fairly beautiful.
They have shopped the foul
alleys of Selma, finding red
hair and eyes with dark powers.
On the night of my birth I'll
proceed to a particular motel.
At an appointed moment someone
will knock two times and enter.
It will be my gift, paid up
until morning, and I'll try
to talk with him first, then
just give up and rattle him
orders that he'll understand
or embellish, teaching me love
the easy way: arms obligated
to take me, repaying each kiss,
caressing by reflex. I'll be
nice to him, hoping he might
contract my desire, knowing he'll
ditch me when his watch strikes
day, anxious for a real fuck or
someone who speaks his language,
as dull and slurred as that is.

10 Dead Friends

for Ishmael Houston-Jones

Cass Romanski, 23, and his fiancée made dinner at his family home in Arcadia. After his parents went to bed, they argued over the date of their forthcoming marriage. He became hysterical, walked into the next room, locked the door, and shot himself in the head.

Eric Brown, 16, was riding a motorcycle near his home in Glendale. He went over a bump, lost control of his bike, and was thrown across the handlebars into some rocks.

Mervyn Fox, 56, spent the night in the pool house at his estranged wife's home in Altadena. He'd looked ill for several weeks. He read part of Aldous Huxley's *The Devils*, swallowed a bottle of sleeping pills, and lay down on the bed.

Bunker Spreckles, 28, was at a party. He'd shot heroin for the first time earlier that evening. Excusing himself from his friends, he walked out to his car and shot up twice as much.

Robert Benton, 43, was having trouble with his lover, John Koenig. They argued and Koenig left. Benton's oldest friend, Annetta Fox, came by and tried to comfort him. They drank a bottle of champagne, then she went home. Soon after she left, he shot himself in the chest. Annetta said that at that moment her car jerked sharply to the left.

John Wells, 25, was loading his surfboard into his van alongside Pacific Coast Highway in Huntington Beach. It was a clear spring day. A speeding car struck him, throwing him thirty feet in the air.

Michael Thompson, 28, drove his black Cadillac up Laurel Canyon Boulevard to Mulholland Drive. He pulled off the road at a remote spot, left the motor running, and lay down across the backseat, sucking a hose that he'd attached to the tailpipe.

Annetta Fox, 55, entered the hospital for bronchitis. It was discovered she had lung cancer. They removed one lung. A month later at home, she stood up from a chair to go to the bathroom and her legs gave out. She was rushed to the hospital, where it was discovered the cancer had spread throughout her body.

John Flanigan, 26, was confined to a wheelchair. Year by year he grew frailer and finally stayed in his bed. On the night before his 27th birthday, worn out from excitement over the next day's party, he lapsed into a coma.

David Sellers, 17, met an older man at a bar and went home with him. They had sex. The man gave him some money. Afterwards he walked to a nearby phone booth and called his roommate to ask for a ride. Midway through the conversation, a blood vessel in his brain burst.

—1981

Missing Men

George

George smoked a cigarette. He was staring
at a bare lightbulb high on a wall, then
closing his eyes and watching its twin on
the backs of his eyelids. A band sang about
empty lives. "It's about death," yelled
a thin, handsome kid on the stage. "Snort
meth and you die. Die right here. When
you die, you're just dead, man." George
opened his empty blue eyes. He stared and
smiled vaguely. He wanted to sleep with
the singer. Now that his admiration for
the band was deposed (every song was the
same one), lust was the feeling left stand-
ing. So he drifted backstage and asked
the kid questions until everyone had gone
home. Now George peered in his new idol's
eyes, shielded his lips with his hand, as
though a poster across the room were trying
to read them, and asked the singer to rim
him. George's smirk had grown luminous,
holding the whole of his face in its up-
draft. The singer bowed to its whisper,
saying, "Why not?," like his lyrics had
taught him to. He yanked the chain on
the overhead light. The dressing room
blackened, then dawned in their narrowing
eyes until they looked softer, milder,
more like puffs of themselves. A hand
reached out and helped a torn tee shirt

up and over the arms which George had
shot in the air, like a kid with two
questions. With a quick twist of
fingers, the loose rayon slacks hit his
ankles. He was pushed forward. His
back was a place where the singer's
hands rested, its skin almost as cool
as a counter's. One palm felt for his
ass, fingered his anus, and was toted
around to revel under the singer's big
nose, who twirled it, and finally
plunged it into his mouth as his penis
hardened completely. Peeking back over
his shoulder, George watched this with
astonishment, covered with goose bumps
which made him resemble a plaster
statue. Then, realizing how stunning
he was to his partner, just as the
singer's knees buckled and that face
tucked in his ass crack, George threw
his pretty, haunted head back and said,
"God," in a deeper voice than his own.

Kip

"Kip" sprawls in my bed with his
clothes around like exhaust. There's
a smile on his lips, as there is an
undertow in the river outside the
smoke-yellowed window, cooling people
and rushing them off. His underwear
seems to have come from inside him,
like breath on my mirror, where he
scribbled his price, so, when I took
my turn pissing, I'd know the cost
without asking, ruining my mood,
which appears to be callous. I
stand at bed's end and order him to
a position, crouching a little to
look up his ass, where I want to
end up the evening in sweat and a
sharp little moment. He has been
fucked hundreds of times. Naked,
his value is present, and a well-
fucked hole is its presence. But
I'm being too clinical. This is
the flesh that belongs to the face
I decided I needed. So I fuck it,
make the most of the "Kip" who's
available, whose resemblance to
something I own is striking, whose
ass I am striking with the palm
of my hand, whose eyes, vaguely
mascaraed, keep what they believe
close to them, like a tenement
child with its one scrawny talent,

protecting it, as if lovers wanted
to steal it. They want to see it
flawing his eyes with an endless-
ness, which leaves him like this.

?

He's who you want to get rid of,
not like a friend, dead drunk,
with his motor vaguely running,
helping you help him home. He's
simply dead, his freckled arms
out, his hairy legs spread,
mouth open, tongue down inside
like a melted candle. You lie
by his dimly lit body, gazing
into the mirror hung on the
ceiling, over his former one.
Somehow, he's less far away
from that distance. When you
look at his simple reflection,
you see what you saw when you
picked him out from his twilit
street corner—a beautiful,
distant young man whose stare
asked your questions for some
kind of feeling. Keeping your
eyes in the mirror, on the
illusion, you cover him with
caresses, as Dad would when
his body was miniature, leaned
in a doorway shaking with
fear. Now, he's as still as
the past in its reaches, and
your body is flushed, prick
broiling. The corpse is the
match tip which lit it, the
formerly dangerous object,

something played out, like
your eyes once you've brought
an idea to fruition, once
you've carried him breathlessly
over your shoulder, his long
hair sweeping the floor of its
scrap paper shanty town, into
the bushes, when he's down in
a hole in the earth, and his
body, as black as a miner's,
is backing, gradually, away.

The Blank Generation

for Rik L. Rik

The future fills you
in with a question.
You answer, "Death,"
get your face on the
lid of *Slash* magazine.

It's as if someone
unchained your hands.
You scratch yourself.
You break a bottle
on your head onstage

and get popular fast.
Kids like to watch
you more than movies
then they're bored
no matter what you do.

You hate them all.
You speak their minds,
writing poems and songs
black with mistakes.
They know what you mean.

You're not on drugs.
You're not singing to
get in their pants.
You see yourself dead.
You scream yourself hoarse.

ABBA

for Brad Gooch

We snort all our coke
on the way to the party.
We bring the new album.
We dance while we listen.

The band is two women
whose husbands control them.
They do not speak our language.
Each syllable's an obstacle.

They are in love with a man.
He is in love with another.
But they're in no hurry.
They could wait forever.

And when they are out
on the make for a lover,
they'll always find him.
They are the tigers.

We are too stoned to.
We dance till we're tired
and listen to lyrics
we mouth like a language.

What we feel, when we
hear them, is inexpressible.
We can't put it in words.
Maybe our dances show it.

ABBA lives for their music.
We long for each other.
They see what we're doing.
They put it on record.

They play it, we listen.
We are absolutely stunned.
We feel, and they know
more than anyone can say.

No God
for Michael Silverblatt

Sometimes I go to the pornos,
look through films for a face
I remember from youth, grow
distracted, drive the street
till I find it drawn in shadow

over another, open my car door
and swipe love. My Mercedes
still smells empty seven years
later. The dust from a thousand
big hiking boots, tennies, and

sandals blurs softly into the
fur at the foot of the seat
nearest my side, where guys have
enthroned themselves for long
drives, slouched in the vinyl,

having gazed inside from the
sidewalk, like into a wishing
well. I parted the traffic
tonight, prowled for a young
man who looked like a shadow,

saw this guy staring straight
through me, swaying downtown
in loose jeans, with something
vague on his mind. He'll go
with me, do what I do. Nothing

else interests him this side
of death. Like me he's just
moving farther away. I can give
him a ride there, because my
route takes me over his haunt

like a man who, so long ago,
gathered livestock lost in the
snow, ran out of gas, and froze
going home. We touch in a black
car, on a back road, until numb.

The Tenderness of the Wolves

Private World

Boys learn to walk. Soon they're gripping each foot fall. Days peak at dead ends, around dancing. They try to yell until their buck teeth are flames, then sip icy beers. In the same city a man schemes. He has grown from a boy to a man, to tenth power. He can see through small clothing or, if not view, sense. He remembers scenes in gym classes long ago. He hates himself for not wrestling then. There are boys waiting at the usual place for a girl, for a man without knowing it. Their heads are flipped back in laughter. Even when they sleep or space out on drugs, rock music remains in their lives. A black flag of it rules the unconscious. It draws their ideas crudely around them. It is their power. They are animals. The man remembers youth well. His viewpoint so fierce and monochromatic, like music's, that boys are drawn closer. They line the school wall sewing joints with their spit, waiting for godhead. They hear this man's rap and break rank, stumble after. They'd crawl nude across fire, blindfolded with ropes around their necks for a powerful sensation. The man realizes and offers them cocaine, then women or violence, the heaven that they understand. So they enter his version, through lungs and big noses. Rooms spin and highs deepen. They pass out together in chairs, across tables, joints still in their kissers. Then the man walks among them rubbing his eyes as if dreaming, for the world's as composed as a photo, but is heavenly warm.

Grip

While raping a boy
slide your hands
around his neck
closing your grip
until he is dead.

And that feeling
stays with you
forever, knowing
you used what he
had then undid it.

Now let the news-
papers take over
and show you
his past and its
promise, his power.

He increases in
value with death
until all young
girls clutch pens
rhyming tributes,

until women kneel
folding up hands,
until even the ones
who despised him
desire him, press

palms into crotches,
his damp open hands
holding onto the girls,
being held on the earth
in a powerful grip.

Darkens

He orbits a hobby horse laughing. His life catches the overhead light. He spins so fast the wind keeps him clean. There is a kid who likes watching him. He is the boyfriend of someone important. He would be missed in a minute. There is a wife in his tarot cards. His breakfast table is well overstocked, the food bright as headlights aimed up. Now his body fills out like his father's. He towers over his schoolmates. They meet him then ache through their bodies. They want to be where love's leashed to the cross-bars. They want to see it transferred to friendship, to lust or a trophy. There is a worn-out ex-boy, mid-admirers. I am that man, looking backwards. I can't explain my attraction. Need love, love power, seek children. And one shines from the pack, well lit by attention, well built by his parents. I hire him to clean up my work room. I slip a pill in his deep breathing mouth. I sculpt a hug into raping. I completely unravel his talent. I take a knife to its history of power. And then its world enters the river's. He winning that cold blue reward. His body softens there, darkens and scrawls. First he's impeccable, tense, too ideal. Then he is weeping, annoys me. Then limp, cool, unprevailable, dull. Then sprawled saint-like on the floor, gazing upwards. I dump that in the river and he is gone.

An Aerial View

When God thinks, "Your turn,"
light soaks the grass in your pipe,
hat's pulled down over your head
and you groove into the ground.

And then He is confused:
"Did I make the right decision?
Was the child an appropriate scapegoat?
What did it do to deserve this?"

His anonymous, grey head
drops in puffy, shopworn hands:
the palms of a dilettante
who does his work by suggestion.

He loves the glimmering earth.
He loves all that springs upon it.
He hates to slip one thing into darkness.
Thus, when He does, He is tortured.

He is bored, pissed, feeling strange,
His eyes hard to read clearly,
His hips dark with a longing;
a child dims where it's beaten.

He is amused and then guilty.
His lips are lava which has cooled,
His mind as wild as the tree tops,
as dope touched to match, breath.

Late Friends

for Robert Piest

They knew you were born to win the Olympics 'cos once,
crossing the quad at school, they saw a spotlight fall
out of the noon, traced it to the gym, through a
skylight, where you practiced as gymnast. At first you
seemed heroic, but talking with you saw your limits: the
sports world, one primitive concept. You never gave War-
hol a chance. And with all your movement came muscle,
then to that the eyes of dark strangers. Once, after work,
someone tails you. You are raped, strangled, and dropped
in the Des Plaines River. The man who does it feels
spiritual and light. Your friends are down wind at the
high school: doused faces, dim shouldered. Aliens where
jocks fire up taller and stronger each day. The girls
dream of you on the crossbars. They saw you naked;
they can see what he did to you. Guys will never touch
the Des Plaines again until you are pulled out, wrapped
in a black towel, and the light goes on under the ripples
again. Then they'll water-ski. First, friends heard
you had run away and pictured you well lit, neck deep
in blue ribbons. But then they found out how you slither,
a grey stretched-out version of you mixed in with the
fishing. Now they doff their good sense in remembrance,
quit night jobs, drop classes. Grades spin in their
upper right hand corner like a slot machine's. It only
lets up when they talk with each other, your name on
their lips, in whispers. It's simple to turn those to

kisses. While you turn endlessly in water beneath the world, your pals are behind, dating your girlfriends, seduced by your buddies. They french-kiss and roll across the things that you loved, like they're putting out a fire.

III. Blind

'83–'93

for

Tim Dlugos

My Direction

I was looking at some paintings in a gallery. Until the last few years, I couldn't have understood them. They were paint. Now they were life, as I understood it. I believed what I saw in them to be pain, although nicely painted. That was the point, but I couldn't explain them further. The gallery space was attractive: cool, white, spacious, and empty. The man propped at the desk in the back was congratulated. He smiled at me. "Like them?" "Yes, quite a bit." "Sure?" He was sweet and ironic, like I'd behave in this instance, confronting a stranger. I spent a few more minutes before the paintings, then walked out. They stayed with me; ideas sketched crudely on less crudely painted pictures of familiar things. So you could see both—the bottom layer more fully, the top layer more quickly. A cartoon character danced on the faces of immigrants from Poland. I walked several blocks to my car, which took me home. Home was as white and empty as the gallery was between shows, as though something was always just on its way out, another heading my way. I breathed easily there. I put on a record and read a magazine for a while. By then the feel of the paintings was gone. Feeling had given way to excitement and need to share that with others. Conversations were long and full of my blather, followed by friends saying that sounded good. They'd go down to see them. A few had news of their own. One had seen a Brazilian film which "moved" him. But he seemed more worked up than moved. He had put it into a list. It made the top ten of the year, he said. I knew I'd go, but the excitement I felt was less than I had for the paintings, and now I had praised them to death. So I thought of my friends who were left. It was heavy to be in their presence, to be their own kind. I felt honored, to be honest. I looked in their eyes when they spoke, which were dilated and bright for reasons I didn't know. But it felt cool to look in them, and better to sit nonchalantly before them as they talked articulately. I recognized how I must have seemed to them several days before, in so many words. Then I walked home. On the way there I stopped in a bakery and bought several pastries, guzzling them at a small table provided. Eating them was sort of like playing with toys. The clerk smiled when she saw me. My pleasure was obvious. "Enjoying them?" "Yes." Then she went back to her job. She was helping somebody else. Our eyes didn't meet again until I walked out the door, and then just to see if I'd paid. Still, they were good. But I never thought of them afterward, sat in a chair, then in the bathtub, then in my bed reading a book from the country where they were invented. France, a place that was art itself. It held a strange attraction for me, not having visited it. One of my friends spent a year painting there. He made it so real. Its colors still glowed eighty years after they were brushed on, and in the cool, derivative paintings by friends who'd only seen reproductions of what they admired in their idols. There was a point they would reach when they'd go beyond that. In a different direction. I hoped I could follow them. I closed my eyes and imagined. That lasted forever. Or maybe I wished that it had. Maybe it will. Death's what I'm talking about. Hope that's clearer now. That was my problem: I thought too hard about things my friends painted around, thereby suggesting them. They were a long way off. I said that half-heartedly, but how would I know. Hence, the effect I was going for. It was just out of reach in the direction I walked. Not quite "home" exactly, but also between exhibitions. My friends would have thrown their hands in the air. I put one foot in front of another. One word after the next. And doing so I kept my place, which was cool and white, only twelve blocks away, where I lay down in my bed, what I thought I was in a few minutes before. But I'm never there. Nobody knew where to reach me. So my work piled up. It looked good on the table. I did too when I slaved over it, having had all I could take. Take this as fact. I was there when I felt what I meant. I could have made some money from it, but I didn't know how. No one told me. They put it into their paintings and I was left trying to see art amidst the black smoke of the times. All of the paintings were black, as I could remember them. But someone told me they were nicer than that. It was so long ago I couldn't remember. A light rain pelted the windows. I sat up in bed and looked at them closely, closed them up. Or night did it for me. Or I finally put me away for good. That was me you heard crying last night. Okay, not crying. But it was me that you heard. I heard I could sleep here.

Love Come Down

for Chris Lemmerhirt

Someone said Randy had gassed himself late Sunday.
He hung around the outskirts of my scene, a better
friend of Kevin's than mine. We were too cool:
"He'd always been on the edge," is my best explanation,

because although Randy shot heroin and changed his hair
cut and color every so often, friends and I had
attributed that to weird moods, vague terms buried
more deeply by each stoned-out smile, what we were

seeing when we thought we knew him, well enough anyway.
If he wouldn't sleep with me, fine. It was a pleasure
to be within eyeshot, cotton to Kevin's gossip—they fucked
one weekend—that Randy "never really got into it, though

his eyes did, even as he tried to prop them open." Kevin
shrugged and called it fate, blames the world as I do
our callousness in Randy's case, wherein a kid simply leaves
the same stoic drug users stunned by his death as had been

struck by his face, specifically eyes, particularly
when blond . . . They were haunting long before he died,
though they will never be pinned down now, stood at some
distance from, or glance away, sorry he ever came.

Winchester Cathedral

There's a face in the back of my mind like a
stained glass window that throws its light on
my lines. Brian Winchester's its name. It

is my subject, like "God" was the subject of
the cathedral thus named. If it's hard to
imagine in this time, it was harder to look

at the light in his eyes, though what I
could see there was admirable, cum laude,
literally. One night he was small and cold

at the crown of the nearest church tower,
a star in the lighting intended to separate
it from the skyline's less known, then he

leapt to the foyer. My hand is falling
to earth. As it touches it scribbles poems
lit from inside. I wish they were lines of

cocaine, less like dust on a place I admire,
the window which brightens my room when it's
sunny outside. Writing a poem in his likeness

I make it as light as the feelings that form
in his wake. Just as black men lugged stones
on their backs many moons to build that church

on the horizon, I've carried these words for
a while, and throw them like rice when he
enters. A mechanical glow from my writing

is changing from heaven to hell with the love
that has colored my lines. Brian Winchester
come home. It feels like a cathedral now.

Kevin Creedon

Outside the glass, an old graveyard darkens.
Pointing there motions my thoughts out, as I'm reminded
of love I withhold, though I'm haunted by lust,
its hallucination of knowing, the lower foundations

on which I've sold my possessions: a stone which
could crumble to dice, rolling snake-eyes forever
from some lucky hand. They'd glower outside my window
like ice in an empty wine glass, or the pile of bones

of a whore who was hung in a loop of his necktie
by men my profession positions in shadows, with cold
cash and downers, when I wander by. I wash my ass
in a basin, rolling my eyes, while following them

to a pillowcase, which lowers me in its sights
and pushes me forward, shyly, when I'm dim as smoke
that I hold a long time in my chest, seems like hours.
My body is perfectly tempered, heaven to heathens

who've found that my looks could stoke others'.
The young men in town have deduced this—some stars,
some just soldiers, but all with my presence around them.
I stow my heart under this cool regard, which

I speak through, like an igloo that has a gloomy opinion
of water when glowing inside with a faltering flame
whose warmth soaks the men around it, like guys
at piano bars singing an old song that grows

with the mood it resembles, until they come up with it,
throw themselves onto its rhythm, or under its weight
with a sigh as my body is lifted up on its toes, and,
in honor of their having known me, looms forward.

Poem for George Miles

When I first sharpened a
pencil in purpling language
and drew my first poem
from its raveling depths
it "poured my heart out"
as thoroughly as I would,
make that could, at nineteen:
"His eyes are the color
of silk just inside a mink
jacket, always luke-warm
like his hand as it rests
on the nape of my neck till
my shorter hairs bristle."
That was ten years ago.
My eyes were black pinpricks
in sharp, tensor light
which my indistinct moods
were explored with, pried
open like tenement doors
on their shadowy hideout
while homework, porn books,
and rough drafts piled up
beneath with a pedestal's
sense of illuminating that
which was most elaborate.
The poem is now cleaned
out of power, as bed is
once sunlight has entered.
I see its mathematics: lines
built as an ornate frame

around a skeletal feeling
that's faded from sight.
Who knows what I meant?
With time, I can guess
that I thought and worked
hard, watched my words,
made them bright as they'd
beam, until I could say
to myself, This is full.

Dreamt Up

I'm not looking at you, though it might seem that I am. I'm looking back through my life, and my friend's death is what's important to me. It changed me, gave me this slightly defensive expression which only a few people see through. If you hold the pages of my journal up to the light you'll see contrasting, interrelating images dealing with him. If you hold this one up you'll find my head is full of the words of another writer. I'll say anything, I suppose, that keeps me out of the jail of my own heart, where I might run into my thoughts about him, like the white lies I told nurses so I could stand by his deathbed for ten seconds way back when. I learned my lesson. I just can't see him as dead. All I can see is what's great about him, though that's all caked up in artifice now, and cloaked in recent history's scariest light. His eyes were circled, deep brown, neither friendly nor wary of anyone. Mine are bright blue and possibly evil in their search through the recesses of friends' private parts while they sleep forever.

Dear Todd,

A typical sort of old asshole did this. We were right here and I got him pissed off but I just figured, "Well?" and that I'd see him around. I've been dazed, sort of up in the air since then. It's okay, I guess. I don't know. Anyway, he pulled some shit out of one of his pockets that I'd been too stoned out to notice. I'm face down, right? Death's in the fucking cards but I break down and cry. It was sort of embarrassing. Kind of stupid, considering. I mean I *knew* it was over. My place got so quiet and I said, "Don't do it," but I can't be sure it got out of my mouth, to be honest. It's still around in here somewhere, to be melodramatic for a second. It's fine but it'll get worse soon, I'm sure. So what. But it's like at the end of a song that sounds great when you're stoned, once it's crashed down, and you sit there with your eyes closed, and what you've just heard reverberates for a long time.

your friend,
Skip

John Kennedy Jr. at Twenty-one

for Raymond Foye

John, his mother and sister step from
the black limousine. They're lit brighter
than everyone else by a round of flashes
and glare off the mini-cam kliegs. He
bites his lip. "This again." Friends
of the family clear a path to the grave.
Once they've knelt, the crowd of re-
porters shouts some condolences. John
thinks they're lying, even the veterans
he remembers from Washington. He grips
his mother's arm. "Mom," he whispers,
"let's make this brief." She nods and
on that motion's soft down swing her neck
crumples up. The cameras click. She's
fifty-one. Her cross, breathy mouth
says, "Yes," with the *s* held forever it
seems. She's annoyed. Caroline stares
straight ahead, swearing out of one
side of her mouth. Later in A.P. wire
photos she'll seem stoned out and the
rumors will start. But here lies one
shimmering nameplate piled with their
world's paltry backyard of flora. John
looks at the flowers, his knees, his
nails. He listens to what the report-
ers are babbling. He lowers his head.
The platform's imperiously gray, just
the way the storm left it. His knees
are soaked through with water. His

eyes are left cold by the long walk
from him to their reason for being
blue. When he returns to his feet at
his mother's command and starts back
to the car, his head's ducked. One
hand's drawn in front of his face so
the cameras can't pick his thoughts.
They're impenetrable but they will
not be glossed over, unlike the grass.

Hello in There

for Jack Skelley

The Strawberry Alarm Clock struck
thirteen. The Giant Crab came forth
with its mouth wide open, scaring
some long hairs. I was staring into
the strobe light. One by one, the
band members joined me. We looked
pretty far out from the balcony.
"You're fascists," muttered a guy
wearing wire rims. "Fuck politics."
Why did I say that? I was on mes-
caline, hashish, and opium. My ego
was climbing the walls, buried
under a slide of Nepal, riding the
back of a woodpecker flying backward
through Time, into the broken red
head of the protester, drifting
in space, growing minuscule in the
millennium. My shirt was black with
white speckles—still is, and my
former girlfriend wears a print
dress, sewn from a tablecloth
found in the actual Whisky-A-Go-Go.
She's keeping its ashtrays as
earrings. When I turned my face
from those flickering images I was
nineteen. I saw this, meaning us,
here, today, as the result of a
mirrored ball, how it turned with
the cosmos, reflecting them up on

the ceiling, screwing it off. The
Churls were the opening act, jam-
ming several leagues under the
light show, in this very basement.
They sang that we would be happy
and warm, meaning now. I tried
to sit, a serape around me, watch-
ing The Circle Jerks spit at the
spotlight. It looks like stars if
you scrunch up your eyes, but
they're yelling the same things
that frightened and wised up a lot
of us, when we were a few of the
thousands of stars up at Woodstock,
friends of the eclipsed at Alta-
mont. I'd like to dance to the
music, but the farther I look in
these punks' narrowed eyes, the
more I see nothing, a re-creation
of life before anything happened,
got naked, took acid. Back then
you could make war stop coming by
placing your hand over the lens
of the slide projector, remember?
But no more. So we live far away,
and we're hippies. We lie on
our backs in a rye field watching
the dark sky revolve—looks a
little like us up there, and that's
how we like it, we think, when we
think about it. Thanks for think-
ing of us. Best wishes, Ian Bruce-
Douglas, singer, Ultimate Spinach.

My Dad

Paul Petersen sang "My Dad," his '64 hit, on *The Donna Reed Show*. He did so stage-left, in full view of Carl Betz, his dad in that scene, in those days. Now it's '83. Feelings for dads aren't so simple. Simping his heart out, Paul Petersen sat on a theatrical trunk, very still. A still of it hangs in the National Archives. He chimed out the number. His father had done him a favor. He was his papa's favorite after he had that hit. That's why he sang it.

Things got back to normal. Carl Betz was Judd, for the Defense, then died of cancer. A friend of my friend Lee's friend Nick's father. We all felt sad, said a few words for him. Paul made his peace with show business and joined an insurance firm. "Now there is a man." That's what he sang to his dad (indirectly), Carl Betz (more indirectly), and my father (most indirectly). "My Dad" directed my life in this fashion. I fashioned Dad out of nothing: a few lyrics, catchy tune, picture sleeve, a vague mental image.

Paul's changed. First, the cute young jock with a grateful dad. Then, a salesman with moustache and gold record. Still sees Elliott Gould on occasion. His last friend in the whirl of the business. I feel for him. Paul was feeling me out when I heard that song, but don't get the wrong vague idea. He was a dish but he didn't deliver. He was his daddy's boy, sat in that shadow.

My dog shat on my copy of Paul Petersen's "My Dad." Now it won't play. Makes a lousy mirror. "Look in me, Pop," the lyric was saying, "see yourself?" When I heard that tune yesteryear I saw Petersen sit on a trunk on a darkened stage in a TV show named for his (quote unquote) mother. Neither loss of his contract, nor lack of reruns, nor black of set, nor back of his jeans, nor *I Dream of Jeannie*, nor "Little Drummer Boy" (my favorite song, after "My Dad," of course) coaxes a lump to my throat like that sensation of love three times removed when Paul Petersen sang his smash to Carl Betz, who I'll bet was emoting a storm, i.e., "popular fiction."

Friction on the set! Giant TV star egos! An ergo remembrance that flickers out then the insurance man sings in a voice that's no longer his own. The one way back is a tune like a tomb. But "My Dad" 's in there! Carl Betz, dead. Paul Petersen, doll. My feelings, dulled. Donna Reed, dowager. Shelley Fabares, *Dynasty* (ABC Wednesday).

Shelley's survived. Her song "Johnny Angel" a cult hit today with ironic and sentimental young fags. But I forget what she said about boyfriends whereas I parenthesized what Mr. Petersen felt for his dad, played it over and over. I covered its tracks and now "My Dad" will never locate me out here. It's lost in a kind of grate, as in "frazzles the nerves" when you listen. It's forgotten, verboten. And I am alone among friends thinking backwards, a ward of its barely there message of pride for a thing that's died.

Hitting Bedrock

for Ziggy Kramer

It was 128885 B.C. The sun rose on Bedrock, turning each icy and slate gray home vaguely pretty and, in some remote way, inviting to cavemen who passed on the highway, returning to wives after nights at the lodge. Now a few business-cavemen backed wooden cars out of driveways, heading to work, and the mysterious blurs of their bare feet propelling the craft between axles were spied by sleepy-eyed dinosaurs who raised one paw in farewell.

All was still dim in the Flintstone house, shadowy behind tiger-skin curtains, when someone stepped to its door. Knock knock knock. "Yeow!" screamed the caveman, cradling his hand, not used to the way they made doors in the suburbs (from stone) as opposed to the blond, giving wood of his own modern Stone Age apartment. Knock, knock, knock, but no answer. So he walked to a window in hopes he could see through the curtains. But no. The only life was the faithful pet Dino, chin still drowsily on his front legs, curled on the doorstep where Fred had hurled him the evening before, as per usual.

Now the police arrived to the accompaniment of their "siren," a macaw perched on the dashboard. An officer pinched the bird and it screeched. The man at the Flintstones' window gestured to them and the blue-loinclothed horde hurried over. "Jeez," muttered the rumpled macaw once his masters were out of ear range. "I'm going south for the summer." He fluttered into the sky and joined a V of bright ducks who quacked, "Get lost!" Blinded by tears, he flew back to the perch.

Bigger and stronger fists hit the door. "Mr. Flintstone?" one officer said. "Open up in there." They listened and shuffled their feet on the still freezing doormat. No sound from within. "Mr. Flintstone? Don't make us break the door in." And already off in the yard two blue-togaed cavecops were chopping a tree for a battering ram.

Six men stood twenty feet from the front door, tree trunk on their shoulders. They rushed up, knocking it off its hinges and into the living room, where it crumbled against a wall. They fanned through the home, candles in one hand, slingshot-guns in the other. "Ack!" yelled one officer, having just kicked in a bedroom door. Pebbles lay sprawled in her playpen. Wilma was crumpled by one of its legs, her head bashed in with a stone which still lay at her side.

Overcome as they were by this sight, the officers didn't hear Fred slide up behind them, an enormous club raised above his head. It crashed down, felling three with one swoop. The others spun around just in time to see his crazed eyes and hear a growl as the club swung again, taking one fellow's head from its shoulders, then crushing what looks another had into the goo of his skull. The last man went down as he stooped over a buddy, battered to mush from behind.

Fred stood, puffing and bright cherry red from exertion, his big belly straining against his damp long johns, his fleshy arms quivering and eyes blank with the resolution of madness. Dead dead dead, he counted. Dead dead dead dead dead. That was just the police. Dead dead—his wife and daughter. Ten in all. "Yabba dabba done," he muttered, did a clumsy dance step, turned, and walked to the kitchen. Cold brontosaurus roast in the freezer. A hunk of corn bread on the counter. Heaven. He sat down at the table to think about who he had clubbed.

The animator leaned back from his drawing table and rubbed a hand through his spiked black hair. He rocked a bit to the Circle Jerks tape that came barreling out of his Walkman tape player, through the featherweight headphones he wore. He was happy with his idea for a *Flintstones* episode. He was sure the boss would promote him or pay him more, or whatever they did at this job to reward budding genius. Sure, his idea was different, but that was what it would take to make the show relevant now, to the kids, who *he* understood. He gathered up his storyboards and, holding them under an arm, walked to the supervisor's cubicle. He knocked on the partition wall.

A man looked up from his typewriter. "Oh, come on in, Avery." The boy took three steps and dropped himself into the chair opposite. "I got a great idea how to save Hanna-Barbera from bankruptcy. Take a look." He thrust the storyboards across the table. The man gave them a quick glance and said, "Great, why don't you come by my place this evening and we'll talk it over. I like employees with ideas." Avery smiled. "Okay, sure." The boss smiled. He'd been hot to get this kid into bed since Day One. Here was his chance to taste "punk meat." He gave the kid his address. Avery stood, shook hands, and strolled off congratulating himself. The boss licked his lips and watched the scrawny boy disappear down the hall.

The poet leaned back from his writing. Why can't I get through a piece nowadays without filling it up with sex and violence? Even in Bedrock it was all I could do not to have the police find the Rubbles dead too, Bamm Bamm with a club up his ass. Why do I think it's so smart and amusing to place the innocent heroes of my and everyone my age's childhood in contexts which darken and ridicule them? And now this cheap device as a way to resolve what is really no idea how to finish the *Flintstones* story itself. And now I'm incapable of the energy to put the young animator in his boss's bed. Or the guts. Or the concentration. Besides, I'd probably have the boss rape and strangle him anyway, knowing me. Nobody needs that. . . . I just sat with my pen in my mouth fifteen minutes trying to think up a next line and *this* is what I come up with. And now another ten minutes, for what? Now I tap my pen on the table. Tap tap tap tap tap tap . . .

God leaned back from the young poet he was manipulating. Enough torture for one day. Let his pen drop and face fall forward onto his ink blotter. Let his arms weaken, his eyes blot out work, and pen roll out of his hand. Rest. No more bad dreams of days gone by. No more lust for the boys he can't have. Let him feel the thing that God feels, which is "nothing"—a grand, bland curiosity with the little, then weariness from it all and a need to simply look off into space, turn one's head, and stare without seeing, over the art one's been making, into the black beyond.

Them

for Jack Shear

I saw them once. I don't know when or who they were because
they were too far away. But I remember certain things, like what
they wore, which wasn't anything special—pants, shirts, tennis
shoes—stuff I've seen countless times since.

I wanted them to know something. I cupped my hands
around my mouth and thought about yelling. But they wouldn't
have heard me. Besides, I didn't belong there. So I sat on a rock
and watched them. For some reason it still matters years later.

I thought about love. I think I confused what they did with
it. But my belief made the day great. I think I decided to make
that my goal—to be like them. I put such incredible faith in the
future that I sobbed a little, I think.

I can't believe I once felt what I'm talking about. I was con-
tent to watch guys doing things I could never have figured out,
not having looked at them closely enough. And when the sun
went down they were part of the dark. I just hopped on my bike
and rode home. Simple as that.

I wish I was that young again. There's a particular photo
I'm thinking of. I look seven or something. It was my birthday. I
posed with some blurred, suntanned boys on three sides of a card
table so piled with gifts that it looked like an aerial view of Dis-
neyland.

The future was bright, and my face showed it. I've never
seen myself happier, but, in a subsequent shot of me sitting cross-
legged on the lawn amidst the now-naked toys, my grin looks
more like the one on the G.I. Joe I was pretending to strangle. I
mean totally forced, fake.

I guess I grew more disappointed over the years, once toys
were tossed in a dumpster, and friends' bodies stretched out

before me instead. I remember looking down at each one in turn, both of us covered with sweat and dirt, thinking, What did I ever see in you?

Toys, pets, boys . . . Inside each enchanting exterior was a vagueness that disappointed me night after night. After a while I stopped bothering to ask them to come back to my place at all. That was before love was much of an issue to me, you see.

I thought of those paintings of angels I'd seen in photos of ancient church ceilings. I thought of other boys snapping each other with wet towels amidst the gym lockers at school. I thought of a porn picture some senior flashed me. Being young, I had many obvious lines of thought.

Now I think how those things are so far away. That's what makes them great—not seeing the brush strokes, not feeling the towel's sting, not hearing a cameraman bark out the orders to guys who would otherwise just lie around in a daze all day.

I know because I was photographed recently. A man came by my apartment, glanced around, told me to sit by some boxes, and said, "Close your mouth." Snap. All I could think was how vague I would seem staring off into space like that. I do look dim, but I guess that's the point.

I've become part of the background—head tilted, lopsided cardboard, rumpled shirt, curved shadow—frozen in black and white. I wish I could figure things out, not that I know where to look, except back. That's where the answer "lies," in half-remembered young strangers who still haunt my barreling thoughts.

They've become an abstraction, a gesture, a re-creation. I wish I'd taken a Polaroid of them. Then I could rip it up, because I'm tired of daydreaming of what they implied every night of my life, or whenever I finally close my eyes, whichever comes first.

I thought they mattered. They do, and they don't. They're

very beautiful back there, but put all that feeling in motion now, get it in some kind of order, then try to explode the whole thing in my face. It can't. It's not built to do that.

But they're still there in the distance, no matter how I mis-remember them. And redefining whatever it was they were doing is all I can do now. To sit here and see them again in the people I love, no matter how cold that looks. It wasn't.

Love Poems Produced by Staring Too Hard at *Thomas,* a Photograph by Sharon Lockhart

Drugged Man, Dying Boy

Massaging this stupid back,
limp as a pillow, and warm,
I feel the blood rushing below
me, wild as the Mississippi's
shit, driven by speedballs?

And the kiddo's guts sleep,
rocking around in their ham-
mock of freckled skin, etc.
His childish head creaks like
the skull's full of ghosts.

I open the paintings of eyes.
Their intelligence composes
something thin and unreliable
like . . . uh, surrealism? His
death'll explain this to me.

A child would put one tender,
barely used hand to his lips
and freeze, naturally stoned
on this image, but, artsy me,
I'll just wend my way into

wherever . . . the horror, etc.,
of his removal from me, mine.
Can't sleep at the thought of it.
Driven to understand why, how,
to devaluate Thomas's beauty,

dump its contents elsewhere . . .
until nothing, whatever, a mess
where he used to stand posing.
And me feeling zilch, only smarter
thereafter, and bored by love.

No Future

We were young
and our heads
were full of
drugs and death.

I polished my
body off nightly.
I played my
guitar all day.

Her eyes were
two miles. If
girls are gods
why'd I eat shit

when we kissed,
or I sang, every
time someone
interviewed me.

She pushed me
into heroin.
When I cared I
hated her for it.

Then I stabbed
her. It's like
cutting a pie,
if you must know.

So, kill me for
it. What did
I know. I was
trying to what.

Mower

I find my head in my hands,
especially when I'm alone,
pen in tow, poem at a loss.
The surface fills up, but
its life's at an indistinct
reference point, way out
back. It threatens wildly
from there like the fist of
a prisoner in documentaries
I'd drift to sleep during. It
yells its story over a din of
hatred cloaked in melancholy
I call home because I'll never
curl up there. That's what
allows me to put life at such
a perspective, not thinking it
out because it can't be, and
not being driven to tears be-
cause I couldn't. I'm ly-
ing in state, a variable left
undecided, attracted by love
in the abstract, but flat on
my back in a daze that won't,
can't be deciphered, the picked
skeleton of a once younger
person whose values can be
written off. Its mouth's open,
lost to what's happening to it.

Teen Idol

When Thomas said,
"Love's overrated,"
I said, "You spoiled
fucking brat." And I
reminded him, "Some
boys have AIDS, re-
tardation," etc. Stuff
he'd never se-e-e-en
up in Beverly Hills.

"There are girls
who'd dismember their
boyfriends for one
word from you,"
I told him. He
knew that, but he
didn't know some of
them were crippled.

So I drove Thomas
down to the hospital
where I volunteer,
where paraplegics
with his posters
taped around them
like a sky, saw him
and gasped like they'd
been diagnosed God.

He hugged them
and was rewarded
with laughter, etc.,
from Hell. He gave
them strips of his
clothes, etc. By end
of day, he was a tattered tramp.

We headed home in
my Hyundai. "Okay,"
he said. "They
were pretty scary."
Everywhere we drove,
girls glanced in the
windows and screamed.
Drivers took one look
then hit stop signs
or other drivers.

It was like Thomas
was holding up a
sign that read,
WORLD WILL END or
SMASHING PUMPKINS
MURDERED. But
this was ye same
olde reaction. He
shrugged his thin
shoulders. See,

if he were talking
to fans instead
of posing, he'd tell
them, "Come over
if and only if you're
incredibly cute, etc.,
and if not, don't
bother," not "Love
is the answer," not
some philosophy.

When in the old days I said something too complimentary, it was my usual bullshit, okay? He can please please believe that. Not to say I was lying. Never to him. But . . . Nevertheless . . . No love, ever, fuck this shit, grow up, etc.—what I've learned from the immediate past. That and don't let my emotions get lost inside somebody else, no matter how like me he seems, or how kindly he looks upon me, or what he might actually say if he said anything. He doesn't know what he feels, friends say. And nothing is sensible or kind. So it seems, though I cling to the notion of his and my powerful friendship at moments like this. I hope he never figures out how fucked up I've become. Forever? Don't tell him. That I mean, truthfully. To escape from his life with my devotedness toward him intact. My dream. That's all one can do, yes? This is the thing I must think when I think about him, which I do every day, and wonder endlessly what our, well, love—or, in other words, friendship, not romance, not sex, and I hate half the people I know for misinterpreting what I was feeling—meant next to how I was taught love would feel. Or not taught is the truth. As much as such feelings exist, I believed in their beauty when he was around, and even when he was dancing away from my feelings long-distance, so unconsciously, so "couldn't possibly mean what he's doing," escaping my sympathy so sympathetically, I thought, needing, I guess, to feel love reflected back just like anyone does when they care far too much about anyone else, whatever *that* means, *that* being love, which I have no big ideas about now that it's gone. He won't call. And I'm so lost that a total delusion of closeness, if that's what it was I was living beneath, I hope not, would be kinder to be back inside. Or to be where he is right this second, even by phone, even though that's so fucking unfair to request, so undeserved on my part, or so he has implied by his silence, which, loving him as I'll continue to do, I agree to begin to acknowledge, thanks.

Some Whore

short walk home,
his snout running,
loose assed, takes
my fist for a thou-
sand, so i pay it
'cause i'm loaded.

arm to the elbow
inside a whatever
year old, says he
loves me to death,
etc., but he loves
death, not me.

i could kill him
sans knowing it,
punch through a
lung, turn my finger-
tip, render the
fucker retarded.

reckless, my fist
in his throat now,
face leaky, embar-
rassed and pleading,
zoned, urinating
all over himself.

jerk off, come,
pay, and he's split-
ting, says, "hey,
thanks a whole fuck-
ing lot," like it's
a joke, like he isn't.

Nurse

There's this guy who still reflects
in bloodshot eyes, glasses, and beer
mugs too lukewarm and fingered to
drink from, though embossed with the
names of some places we cruised.
He was The Future, I tried hard to
believe, out of sheer drunkenness,
I guess, since he was obviously a
hustler, and even a kind of in-joke
among "friends." Oh, him. We're
only horny enough to see through
things, not actually inside. Take that
guy gradually nodding out over a beer
I'd paid a waiter to set before him
with my regards. My God. Too bad
he can't open his eyes wide enough
at this point to see who's hung
around, may not care by this stage
that I'm here being moved by his
stupor, as I was drawn to his beauty
once, in ways I couldn't actually
show. Still, he was touched by the
effort in some remote way, I know.

Drunkenness for . . .

Xmas-fucking-Day,
and we're still
right where we were
when he ODed.
He has left a trail
fragile as . . . Hansel's?

As we drink
his sharp face
brushes out of
death's wherever,
thin shoulders
following, six
feet of dirt,
until his grave
is in the air.

His fans are nuts.
Or we're too fucking
drunk to stand up.
Make him come back.
It's not "Xmas"
without him, not
just drunk again.

We're pathetic.
It's Xmas. We're
yelling at nothing.
We'll wake him up
with our stupid-
ity. No we can't.

On It

I fucked Thomas
up, molested him
with my eyes like,
uh, X-ray vision?

He's feeling wild,
then, out of the
blue, migraines
(I caused them).

Thomas is in
an imperious
place, love
life way over-
stocked, his

eyes colder
and deeper than
skylights. I
can't stand to
look at that.

My ideas, my
desires are all
muffled, flat.
Lead-colored eyes
dirty my view,

and, thus, lessen
all I love. Like
Midas, all exquis-
iteness bugs me.

So I screw Thomas
up, make him less
unbelievable, a
total slut, fucked.

Hand in Glove

One word subtracted from ten
becomes art in a writer's
lofty terms, in this frieze
where a poet can hide what he
mussed. It should be a guy
being fucked on an unmade bed
but in fact it's an old phrase
by which I'm reporting the
cooled interactions that come
into focus now that I'm shield-
ing my eyes from a lust that's
supposed to be ultimate, im-
posing more or less on these
words without growing monot-
onous, godlike. "I lie in a
bed post-drugged-sex," starts
whatever I'm trying to write.
It's "great" to restate this.
Though I'm blind, it is in
my hand, yes? Meaning a work
that's supposed to be filled
up with lust, but couldn't.
I grow too bored, am restrained
if I think about who's ly-
ing outside my grasp . . . I can't
finish. But I've made up my
mind about art, its lasting
effect. It's polished, having
once in the dark been poured
gradually into my body of work
from an impossible height.